Nuances *of* New York

A TRAVEL PHOTO ART BOOK

LAINE CUNNINGHAM

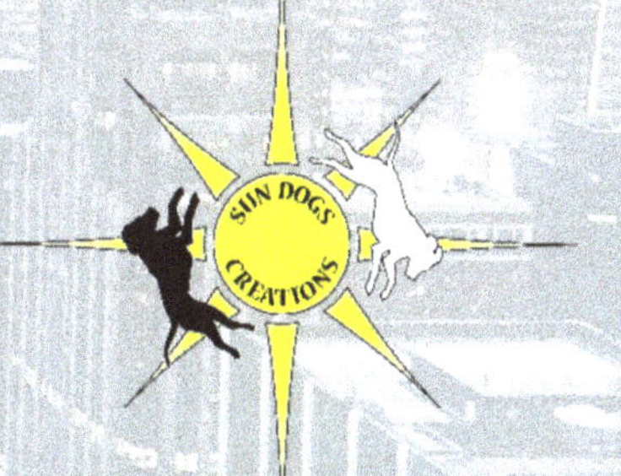

Nuances of New York
A Travel Photo Art Book

Published by Sun Dogs Creations
Changing the World One Book at a Time
ISBN: 9781946732583

Cover Design by Angel Leya

Introduction

As one of the most heavily populated metropolises in the United States, New York City also has a powerful impact worldwide. The influence its citizens exert in art, finance, research, technology, education and entertainment reaches around the globe.

Within New York City are five boroughs, each of which maintains its own unique flavor. Brooklyn, Queens, Manhattan, The Bronx, and Staten Island were originally separate. These counties merged into a single entity in 1898.

Since then, the city has drawn visitors to a place that is always changing and endlessly fascinating. Some 800 languages can be heard on its streets, ensuring that every visitor will feel at home. After starting out as a trading post, this metropolis now hosts nearly 60 million tourists a year.

Turn the page to begin your own journey through the *Nuances of New York.*

OUTSIDE IN

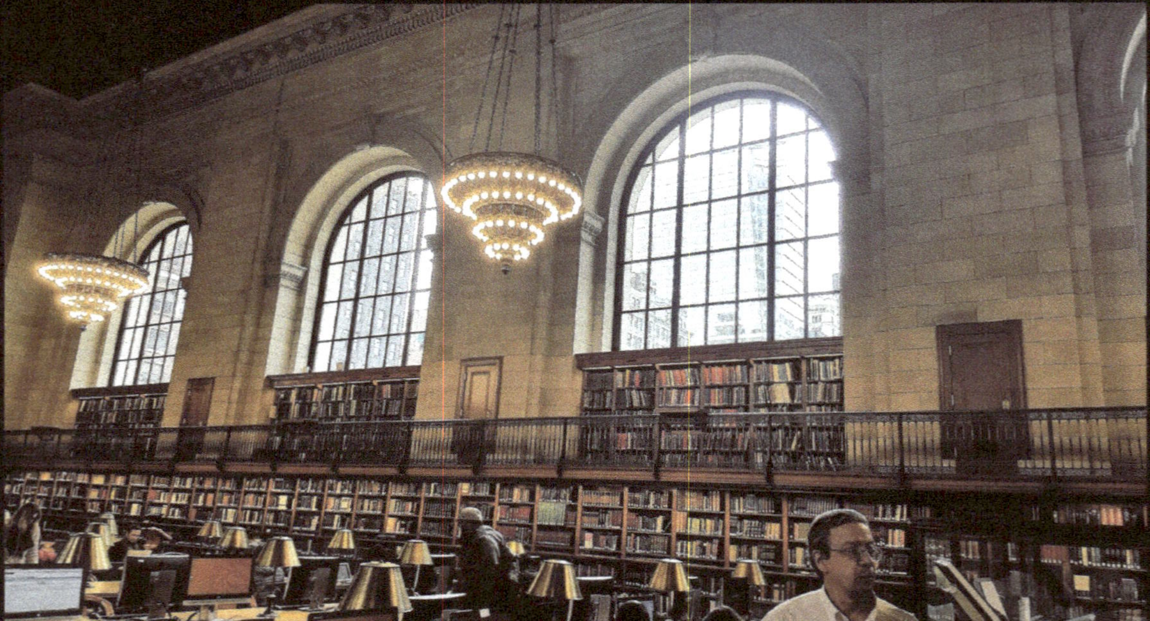

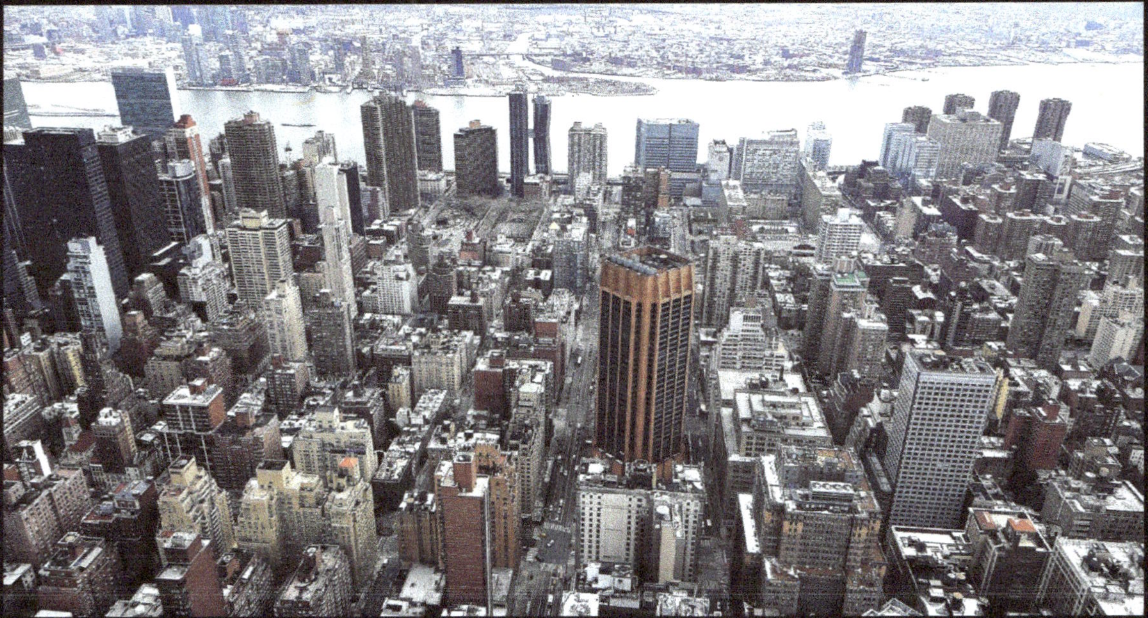

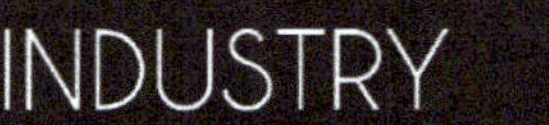

INDUSTRY

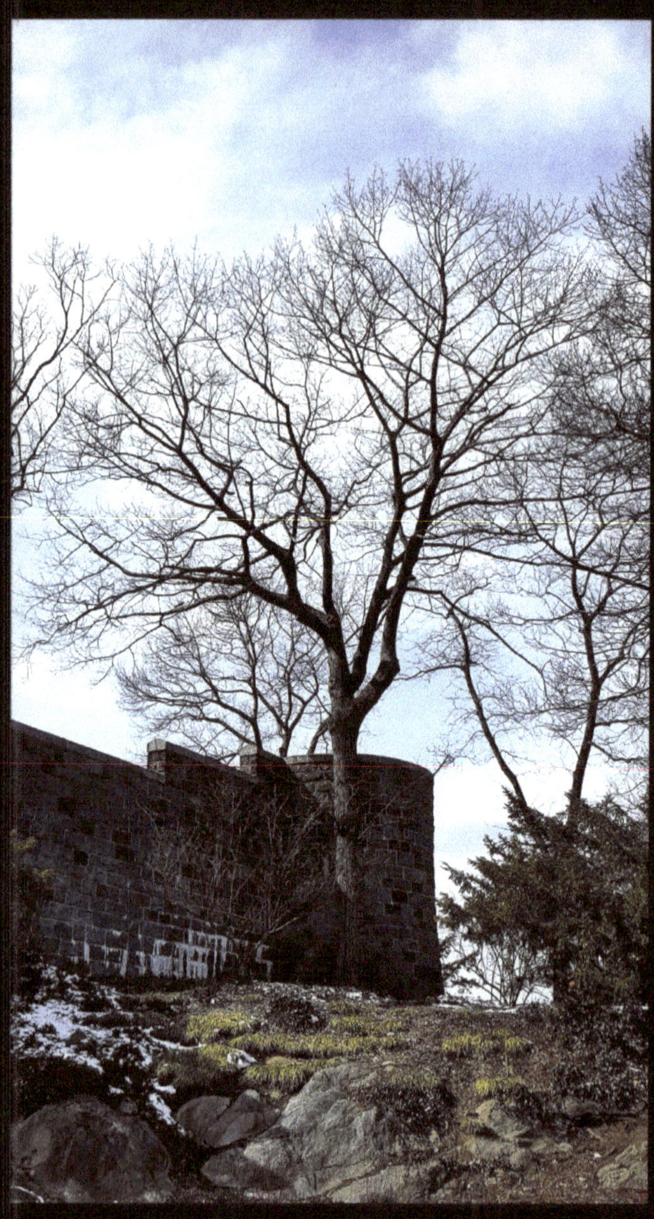

BARREL AND STAVE

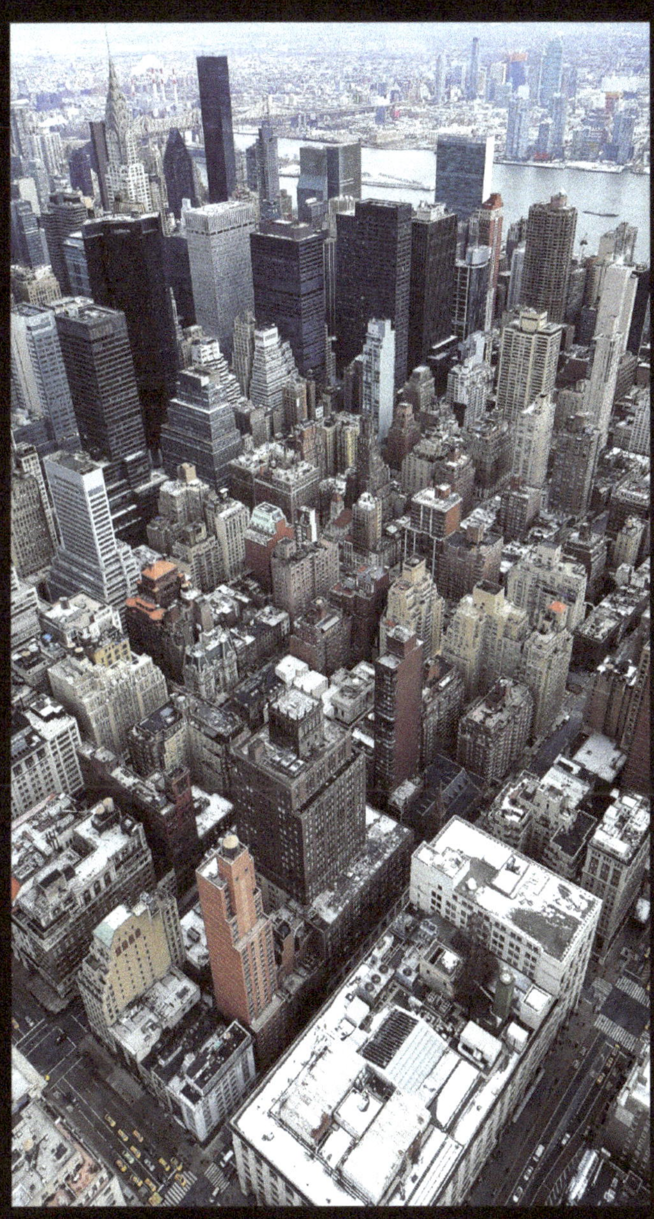

MATCHBOX CITY

FOUNTAIN PEN

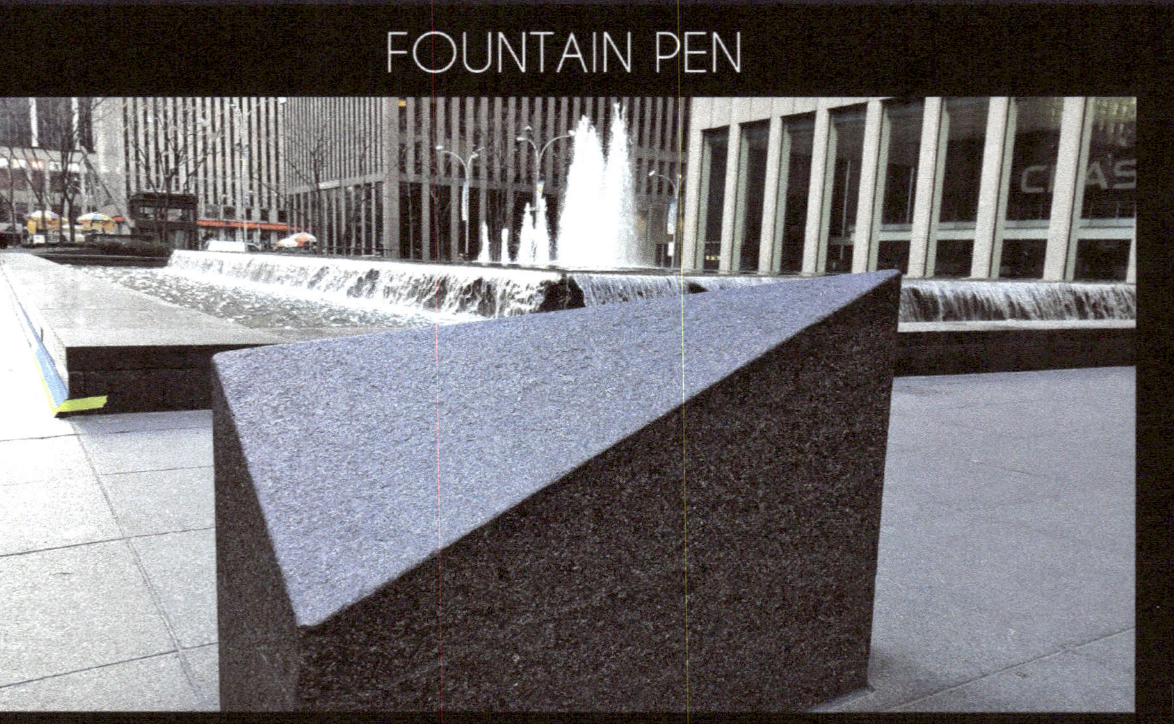

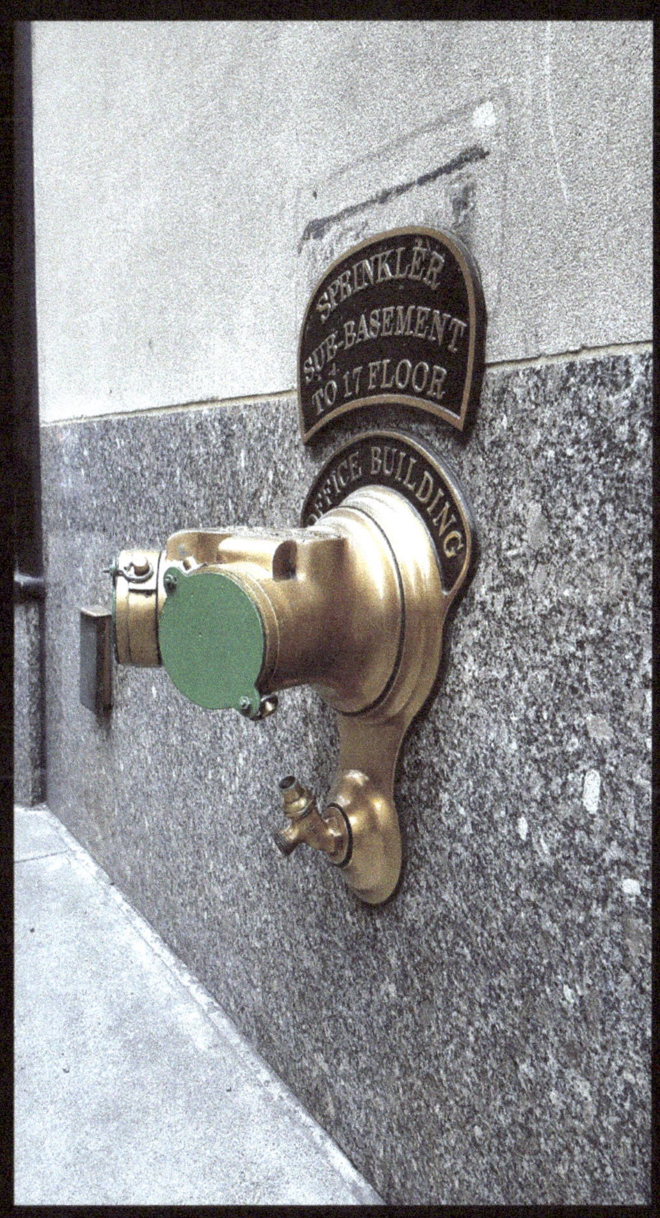

GARGOYLE

LOCKED OUT

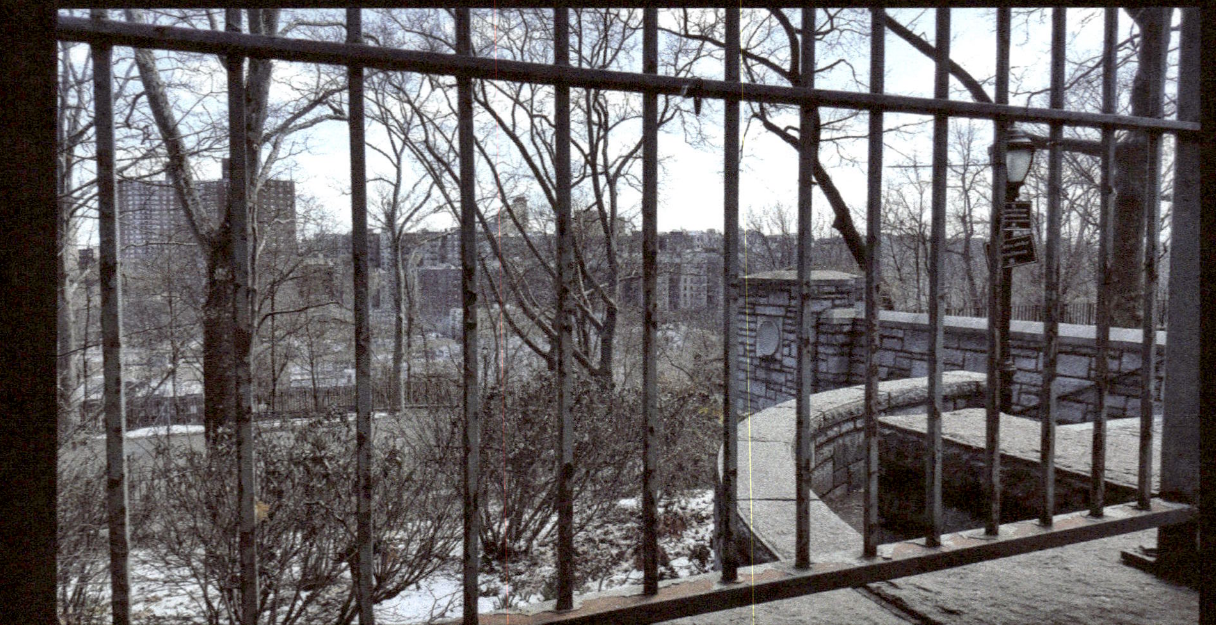

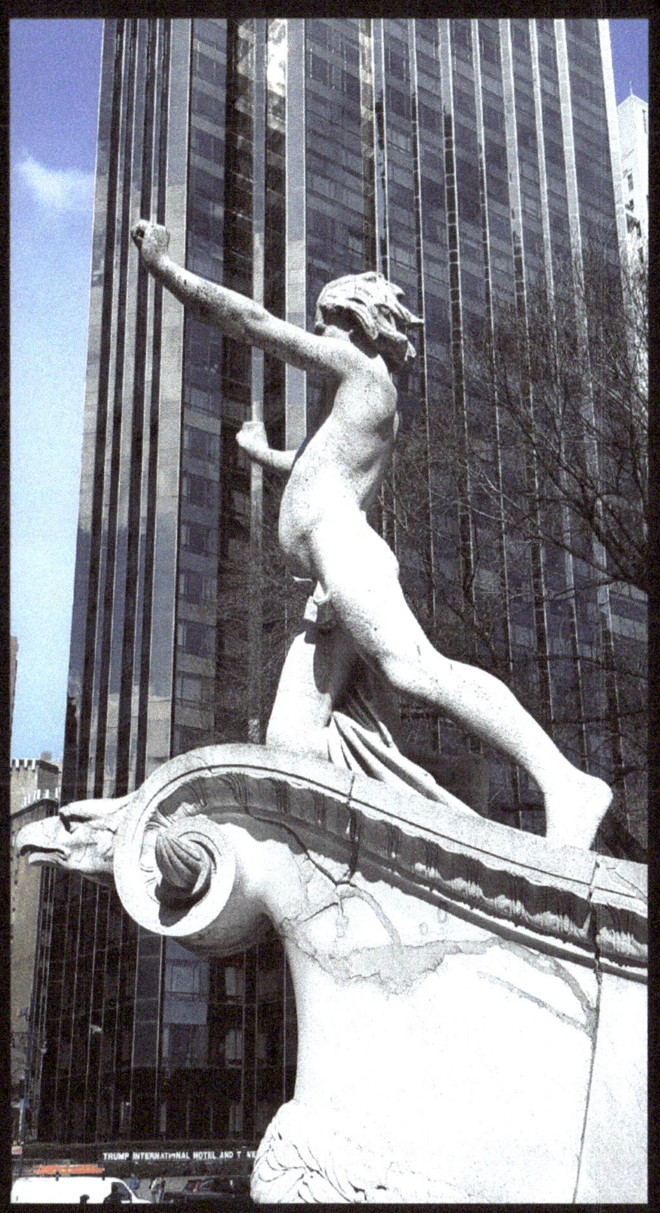

CONCRETE AND STEEL

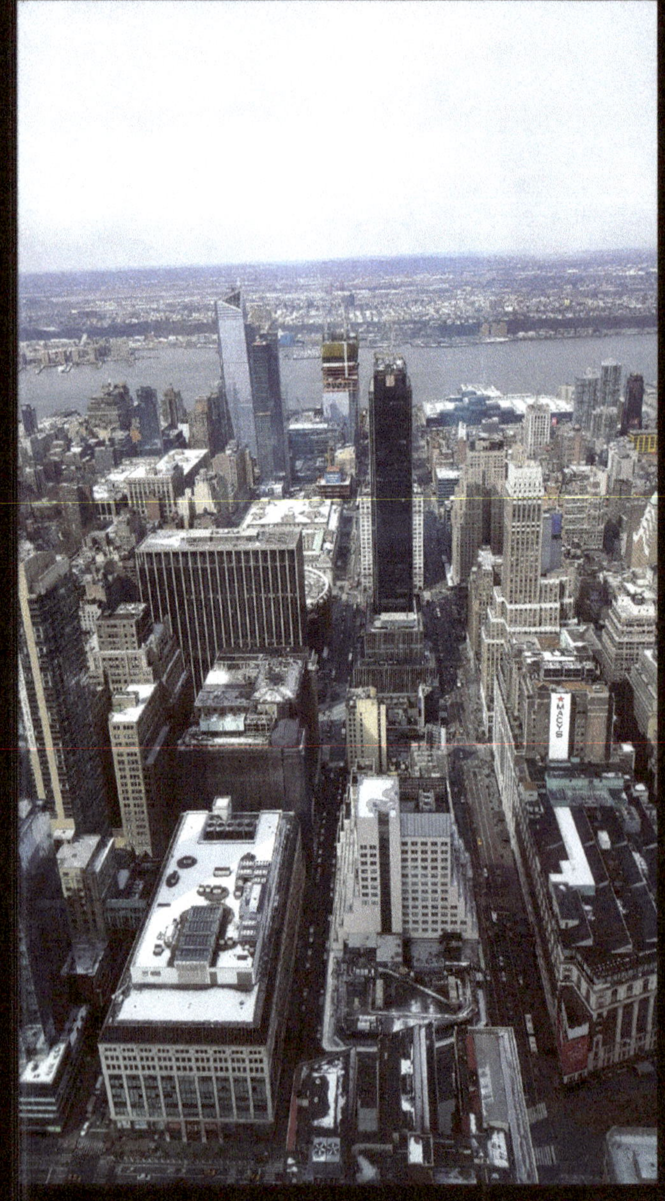

GRINDER

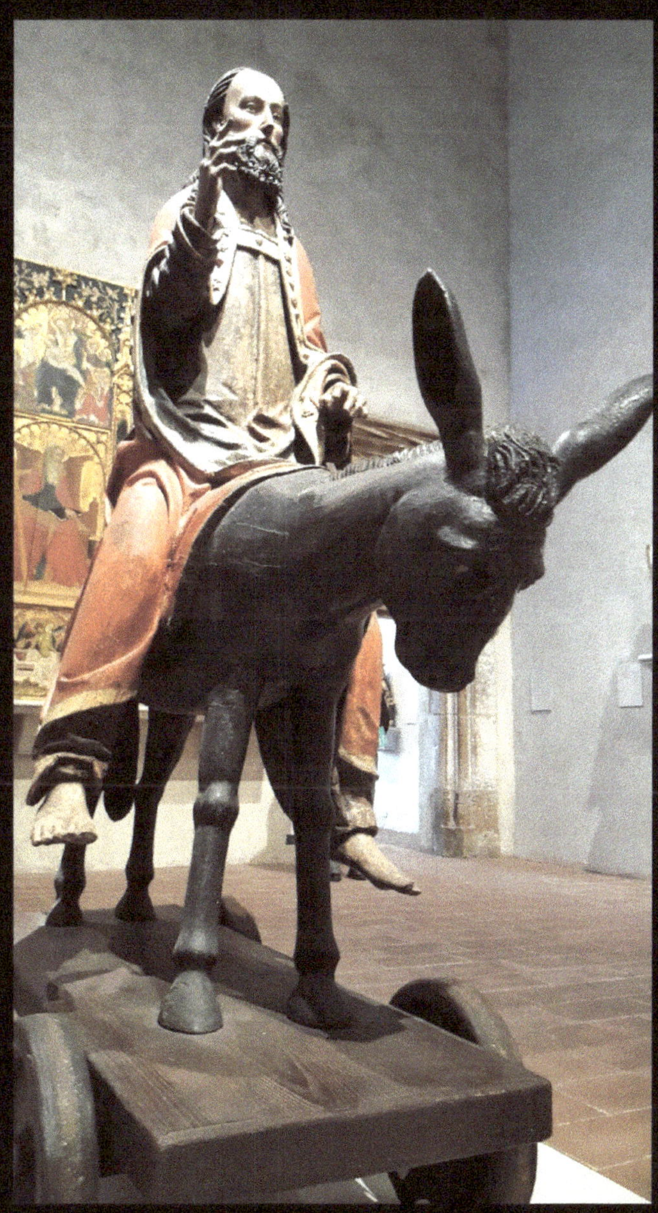

TINY CENTAUR

GREEN SCREEN

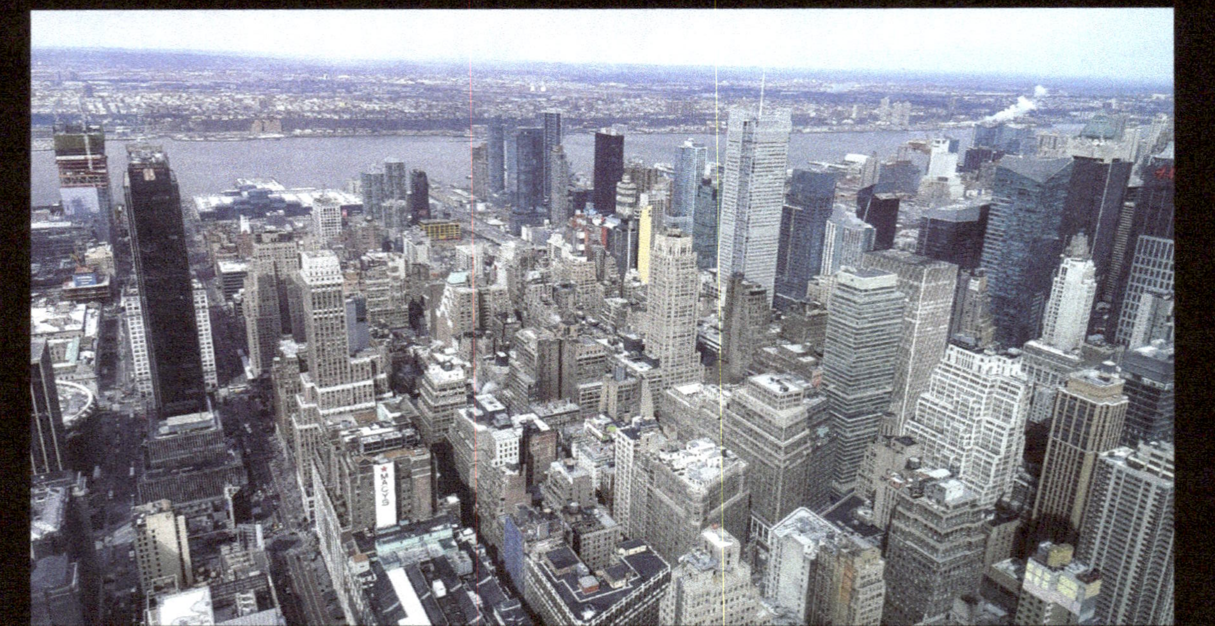

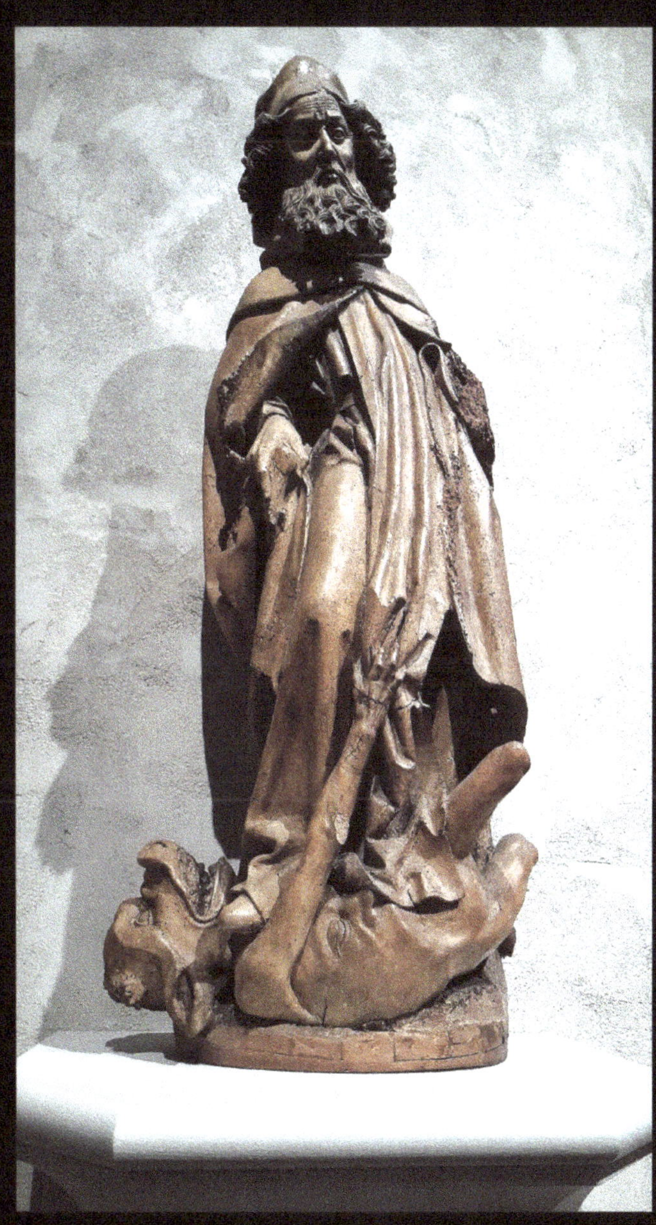

SPOOKY

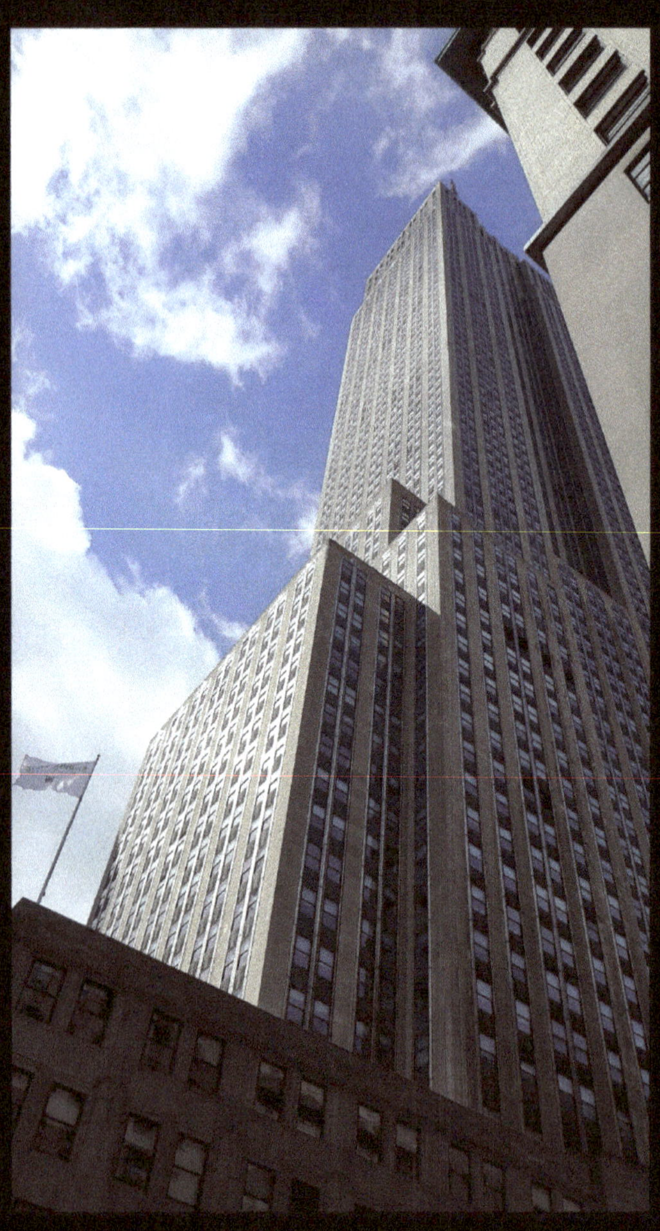

TALL POPPIES

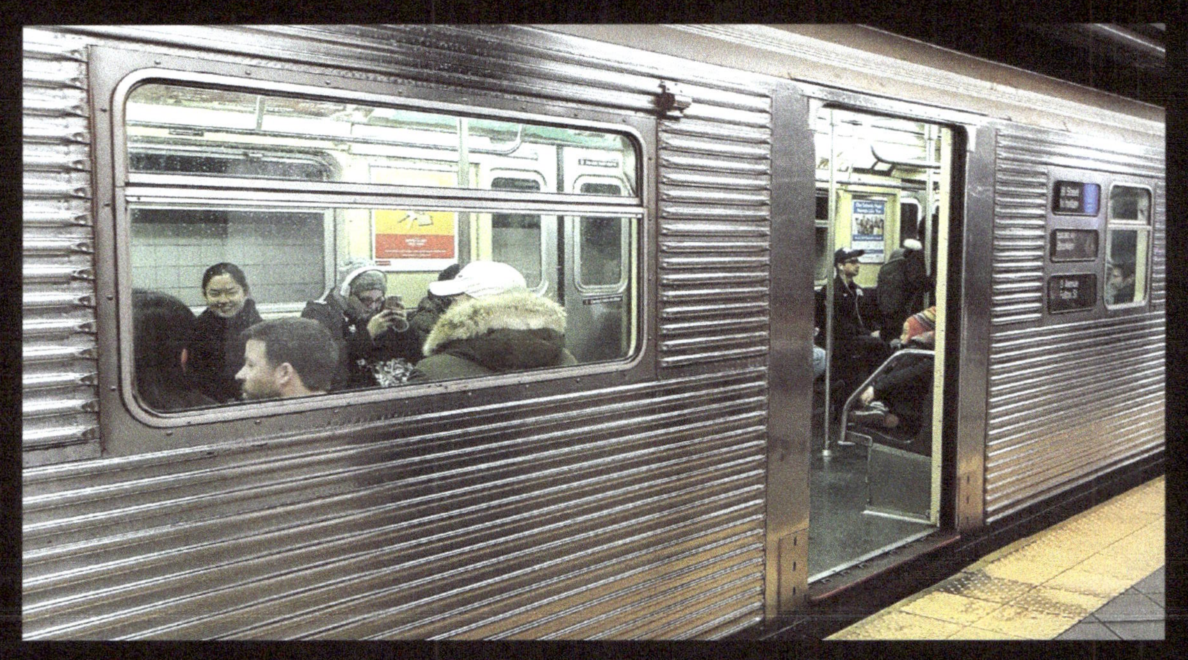

SECOND HOME

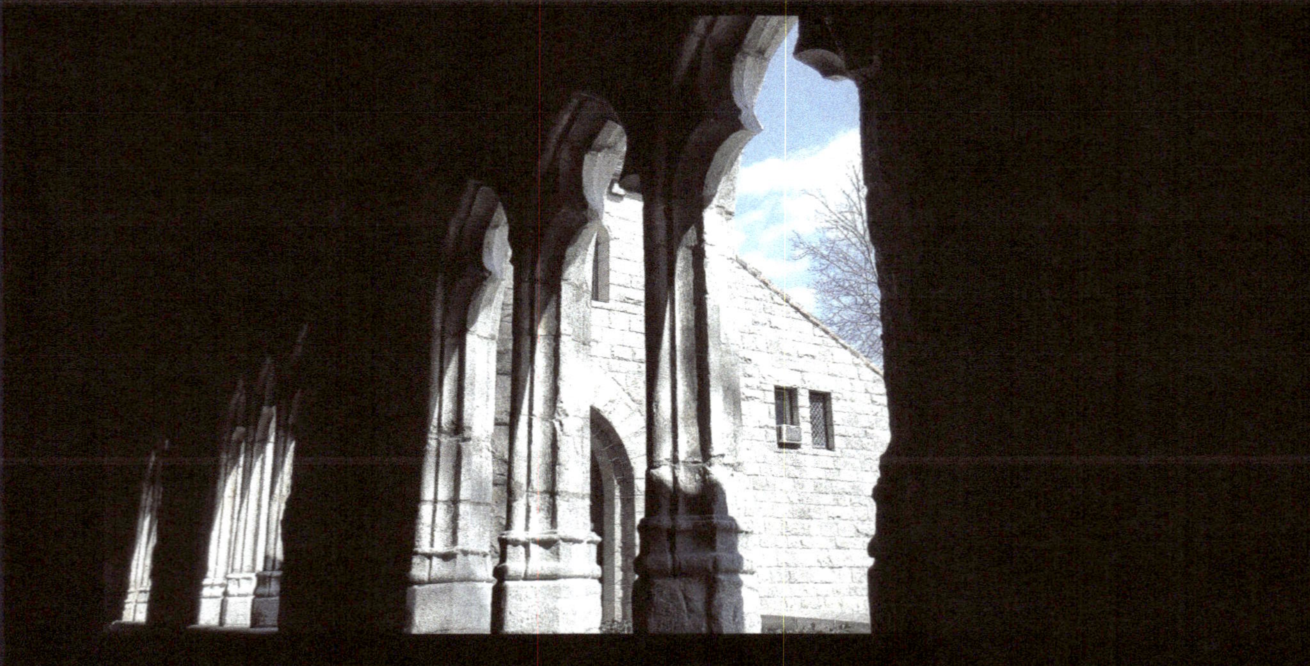
WINDOWS BEYOND

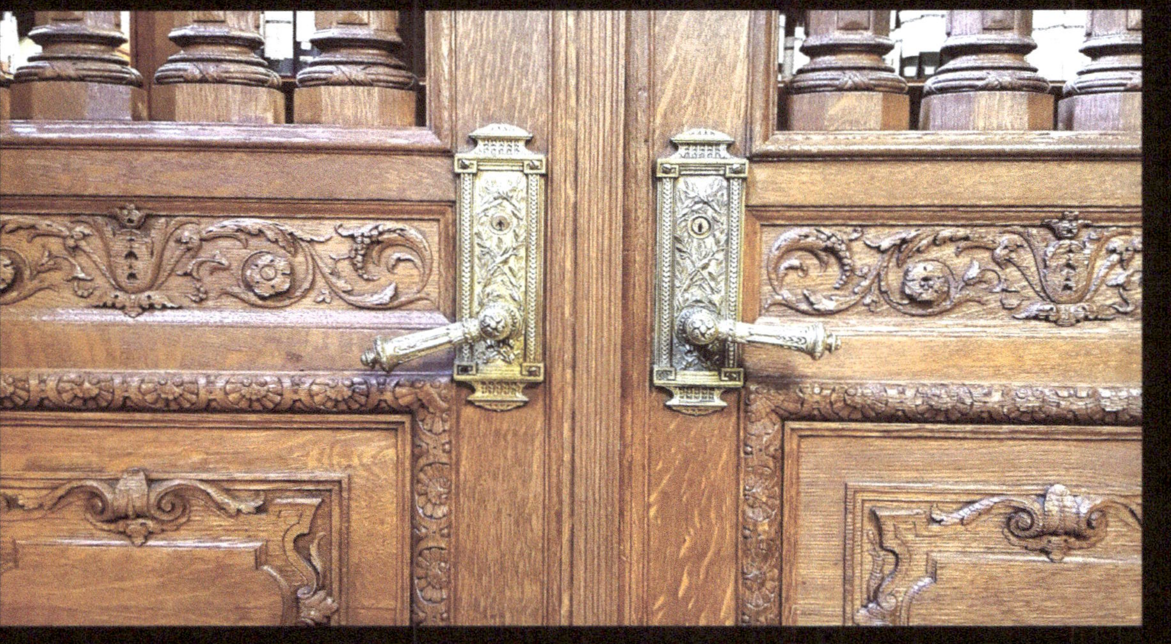

TERRANCE AND PHILLIP

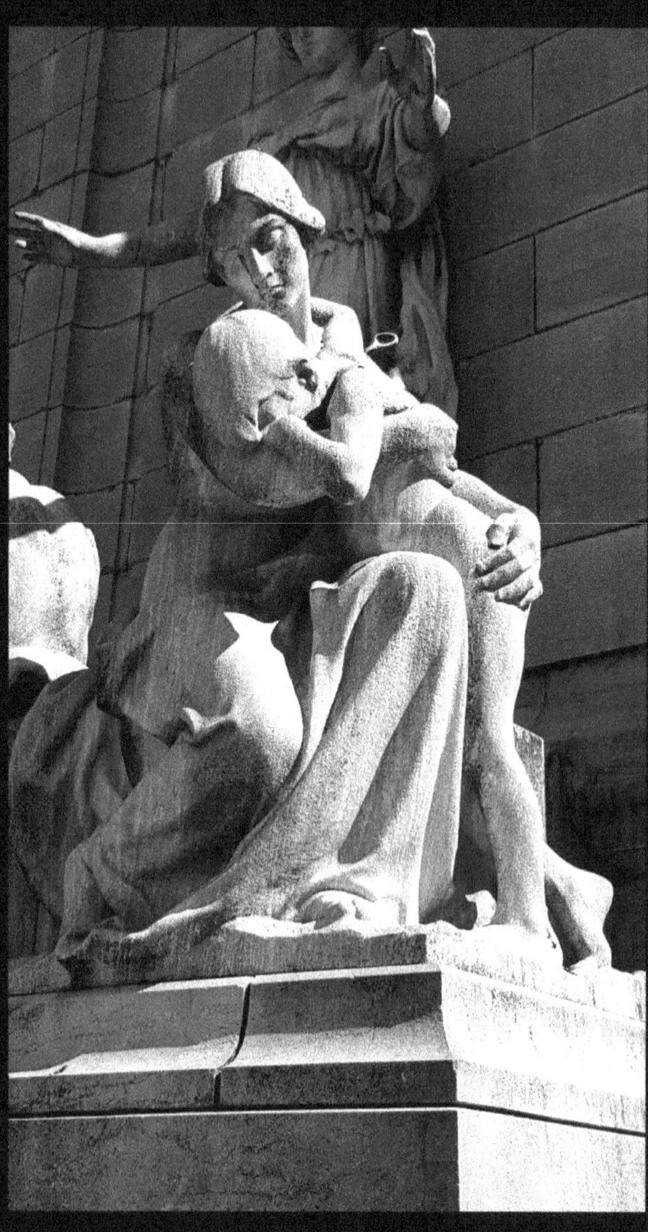

SANCTUARY

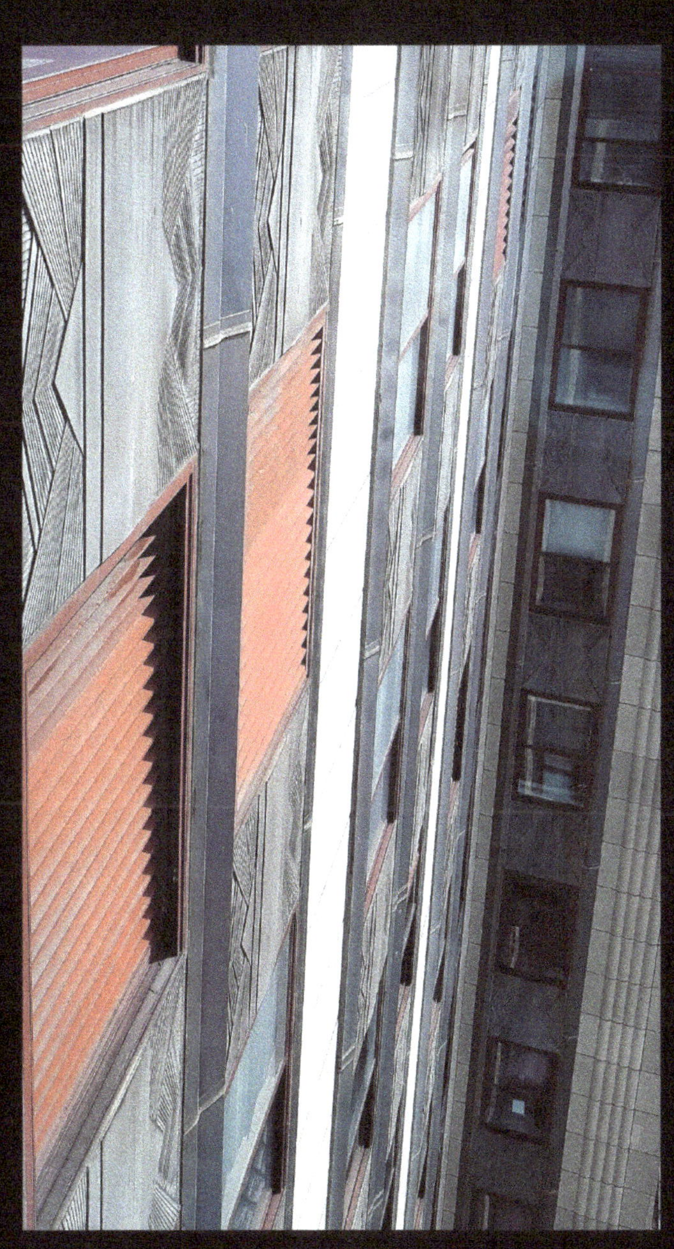

PEEKABOO

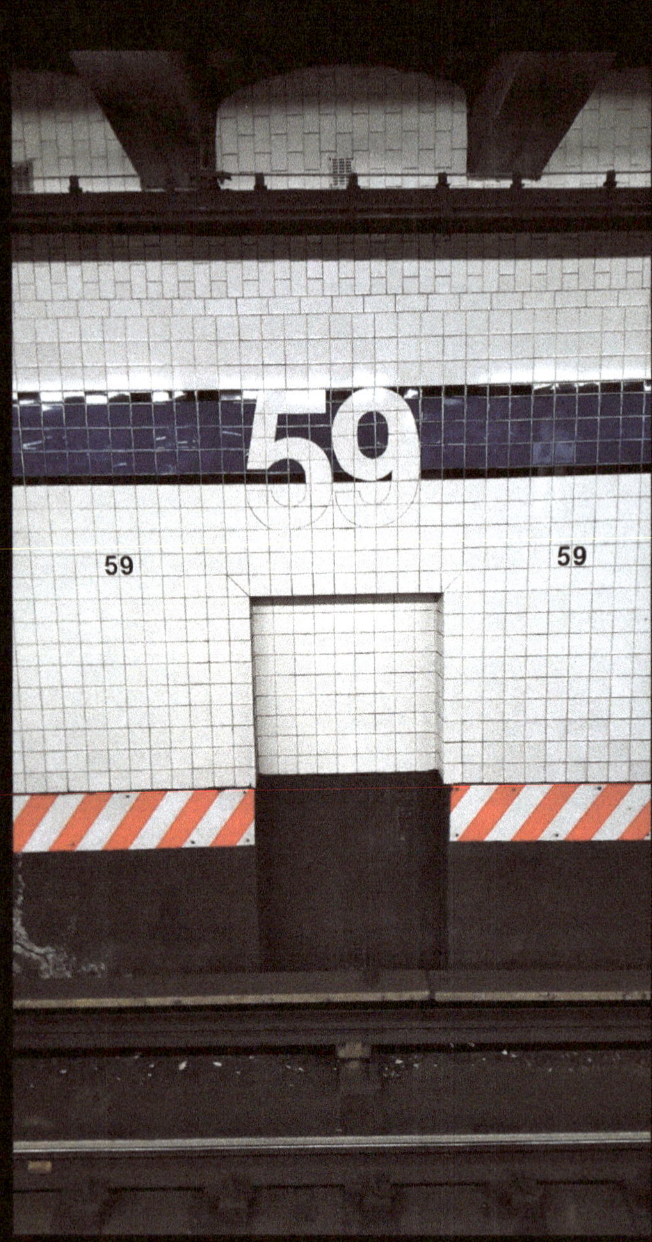

MOSAIC 59

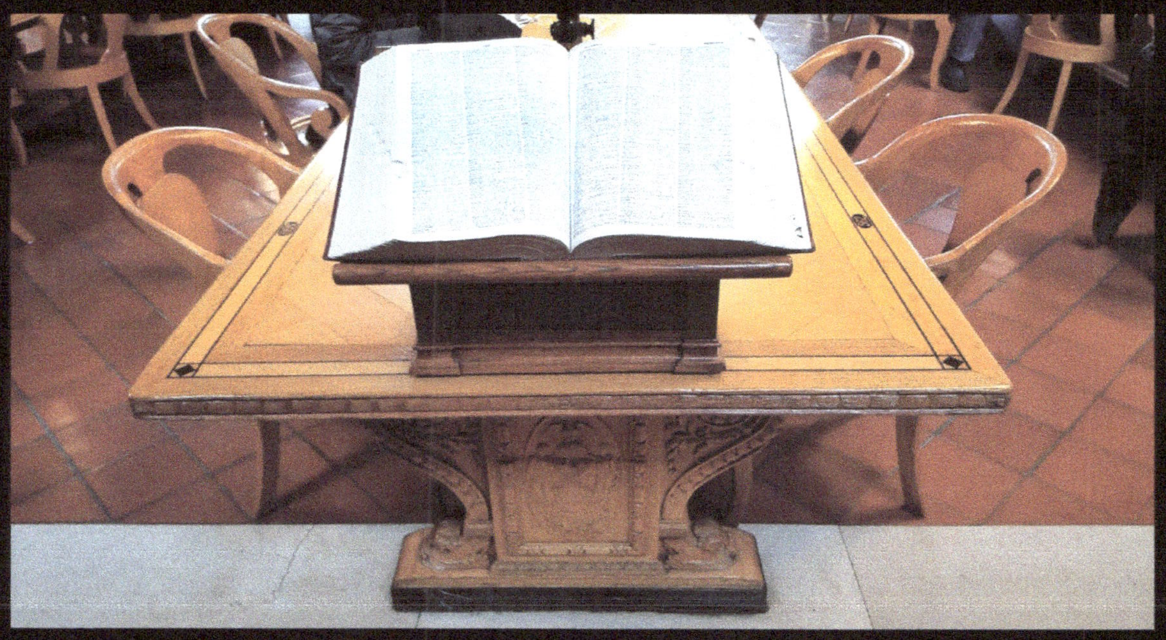

PEDESTAL

NIGHTLINE

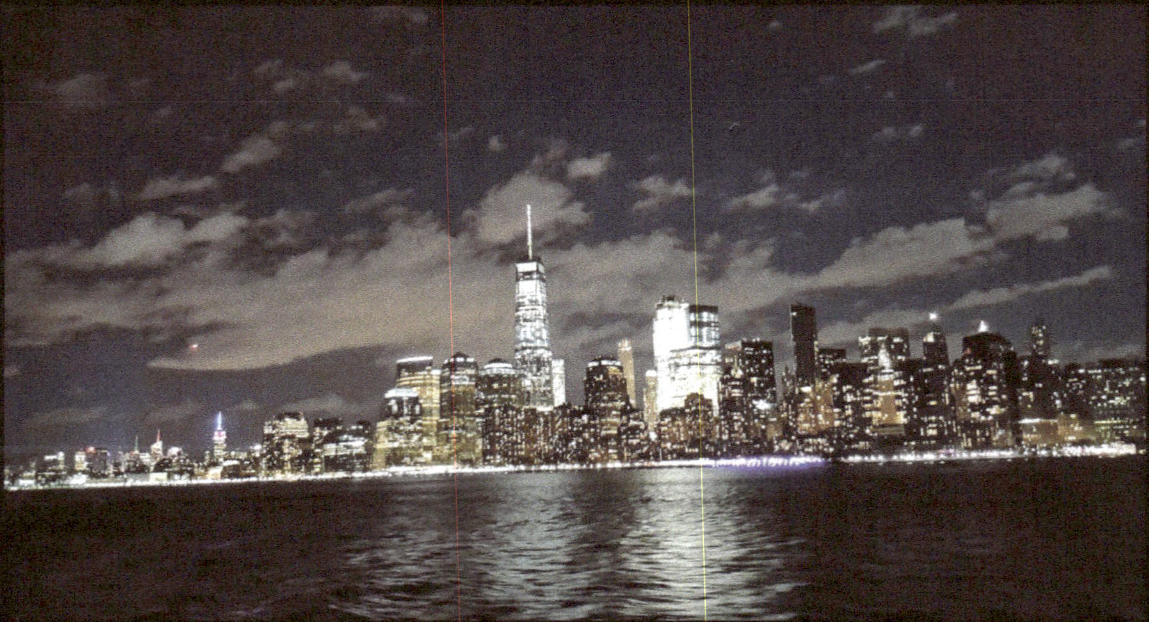

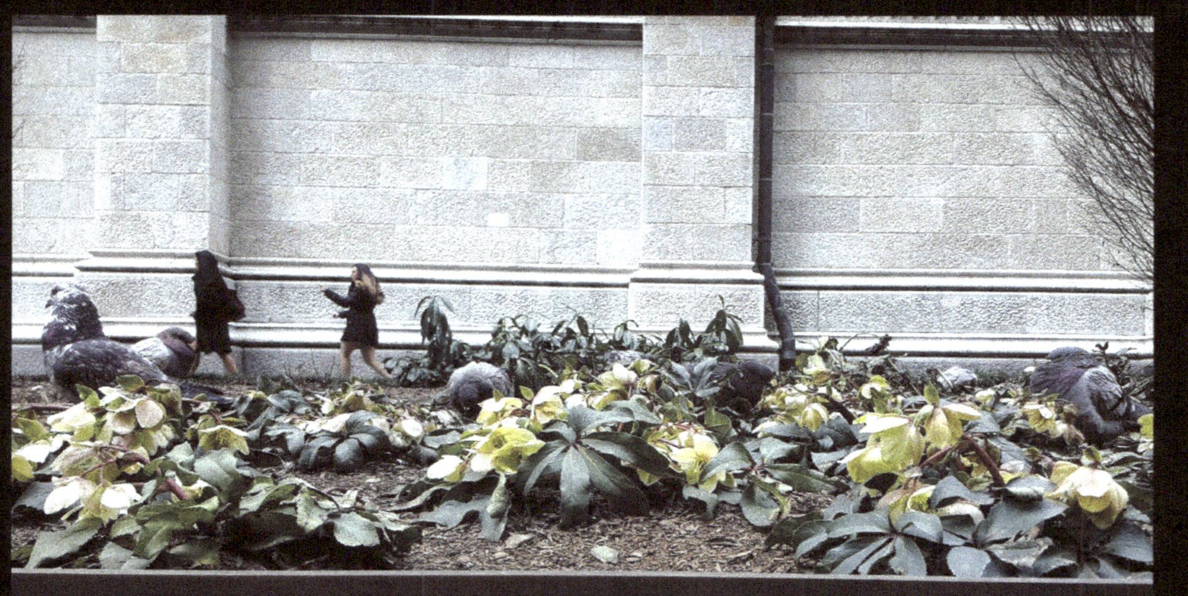

HEN AND CHICKS

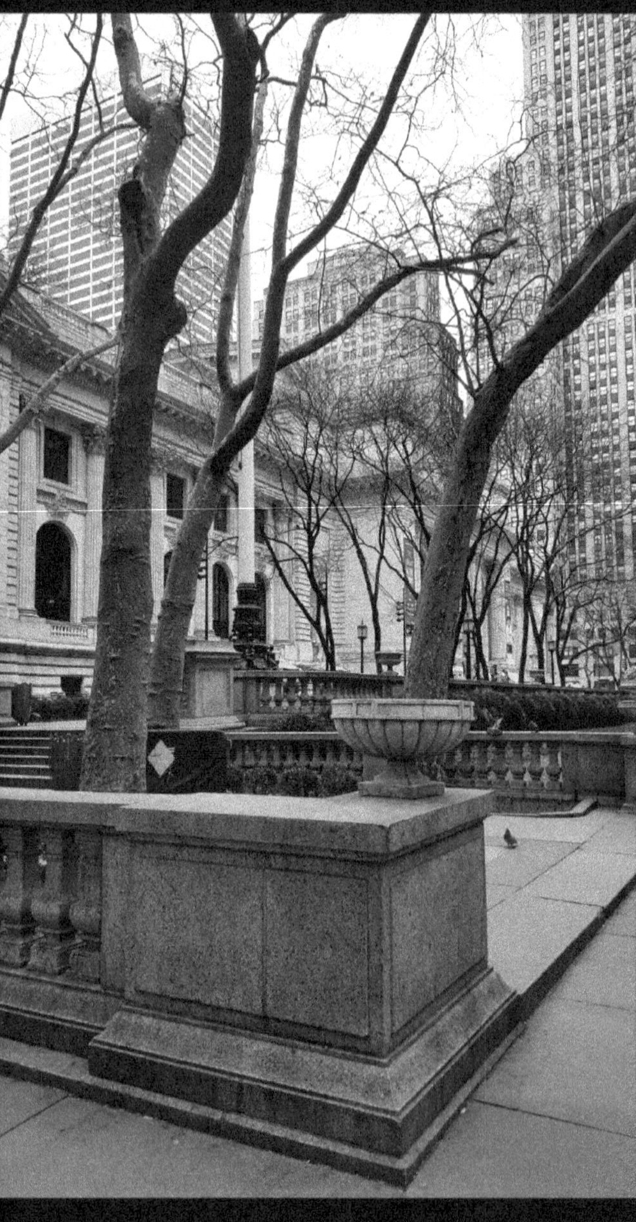

PIAZZA

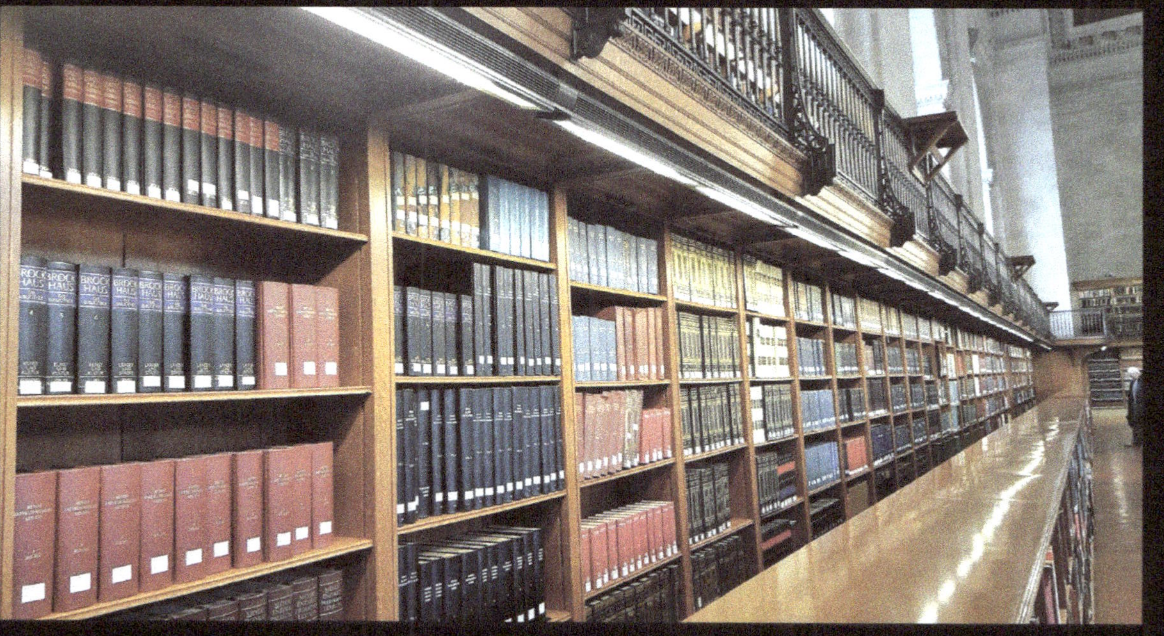

PARADISE

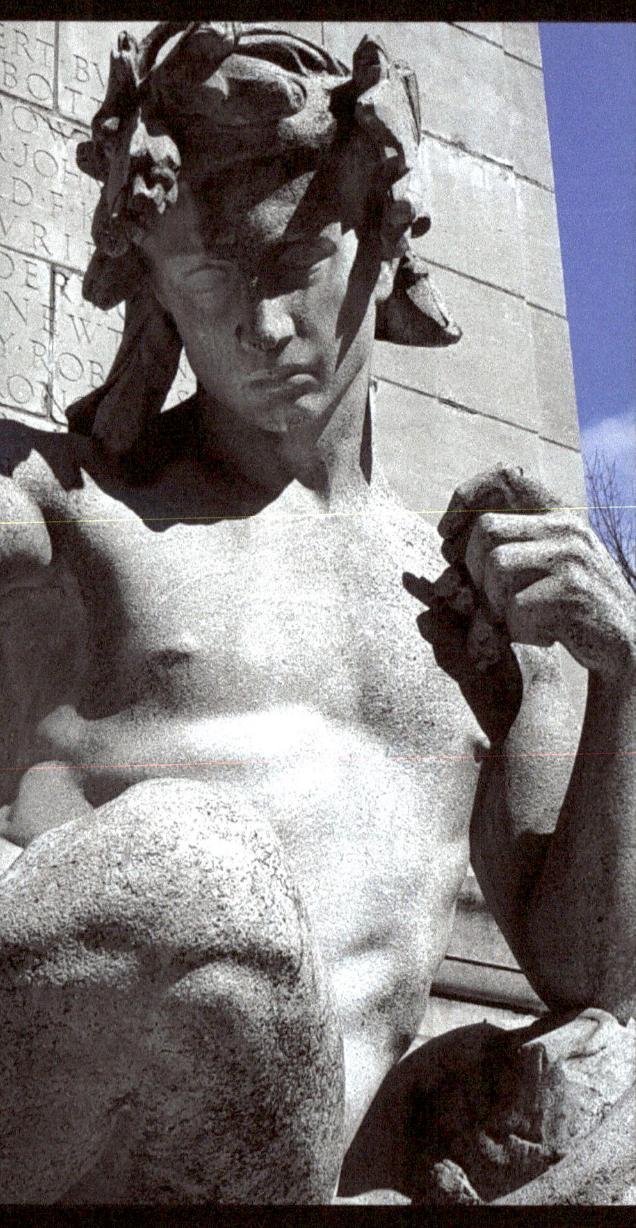

PORTRAIT IN SHADOW

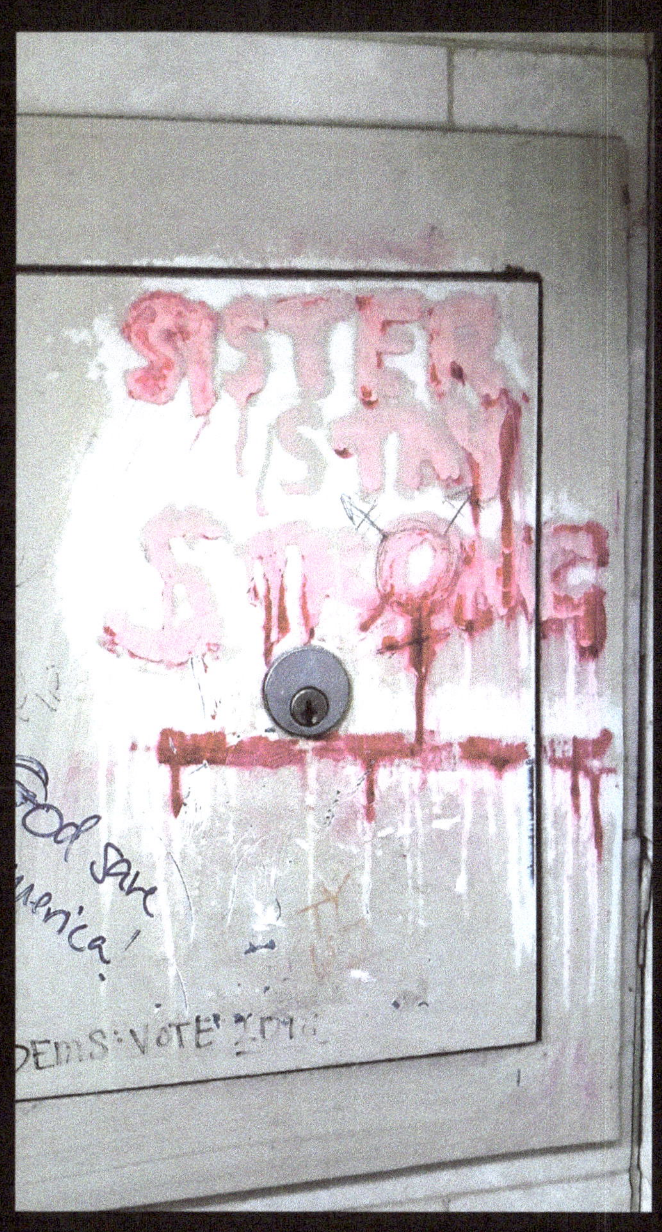

REFUSE TO BE ERASED

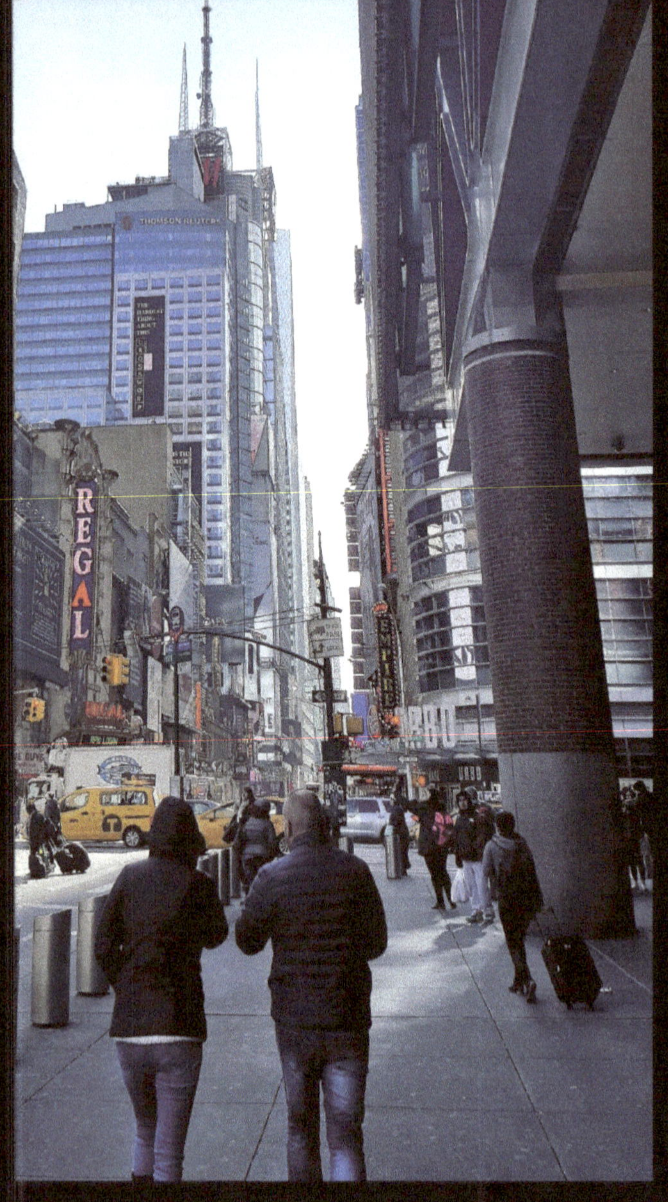

STREET SCENE

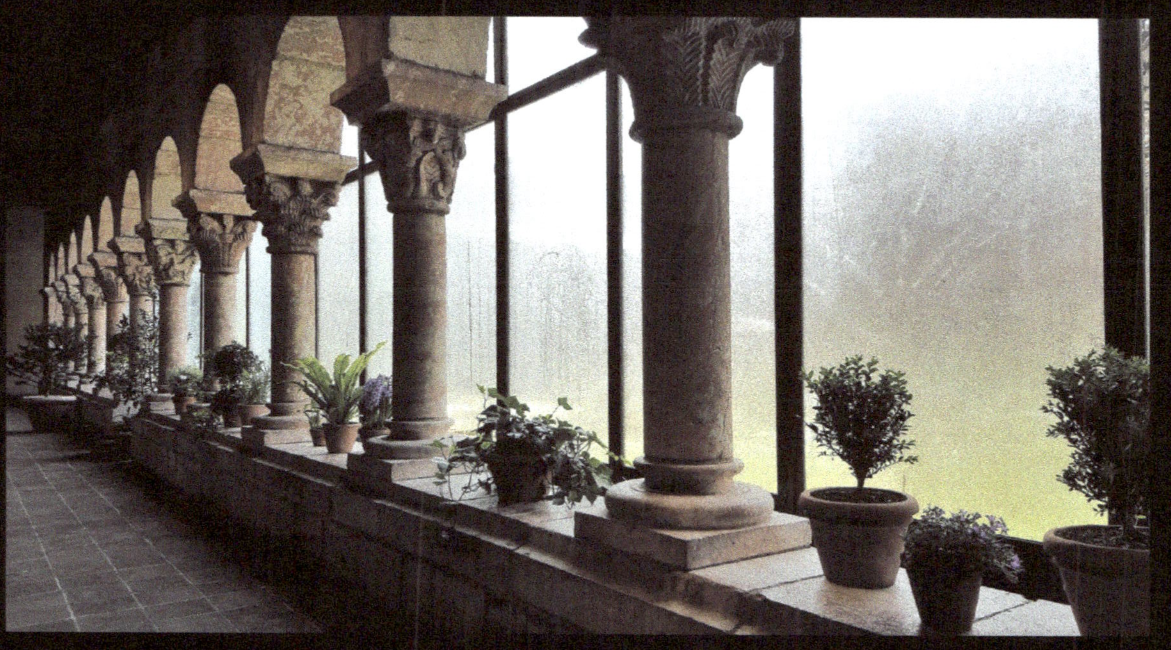
TERRARIUM

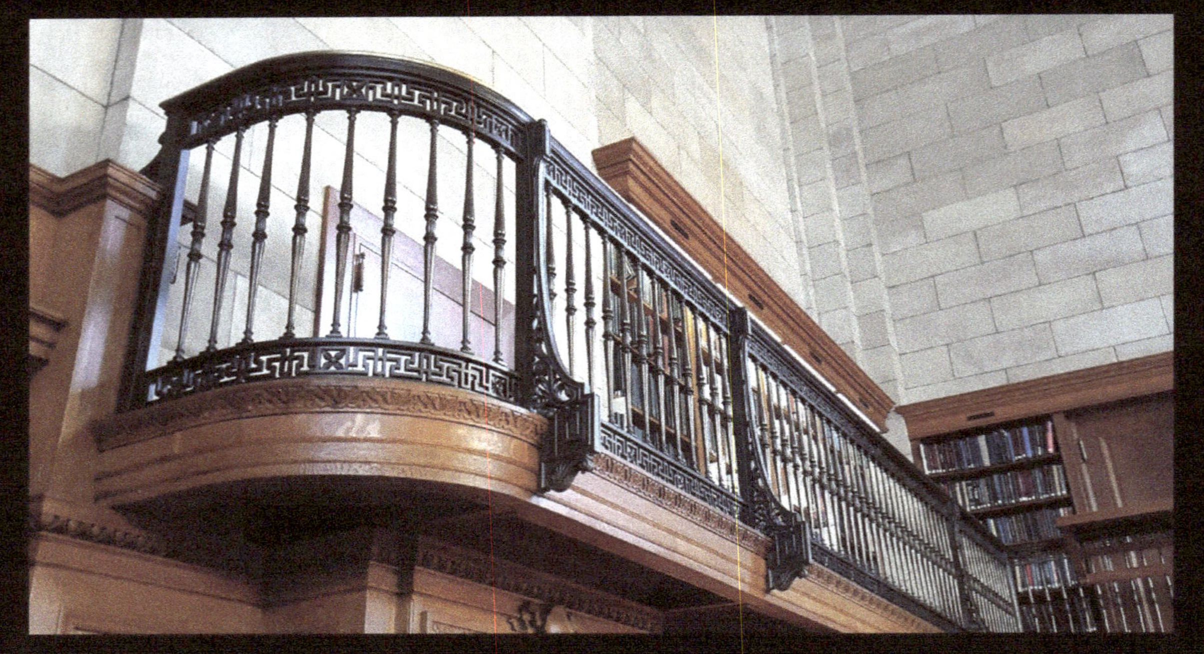

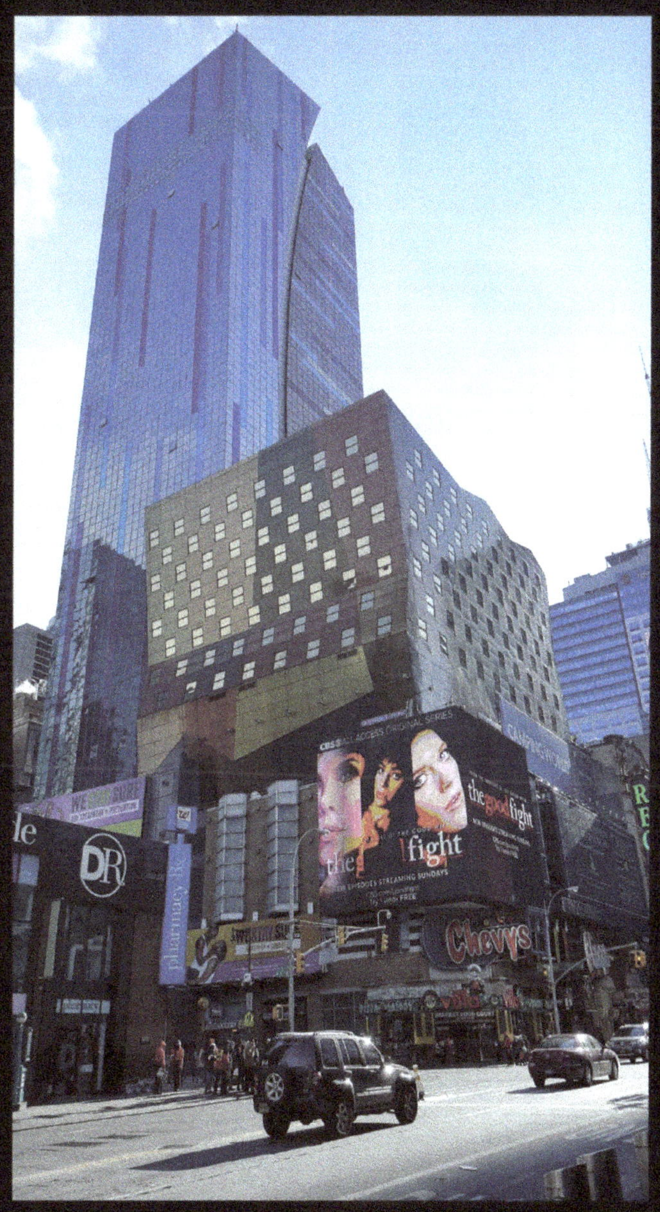

TRAPEZOID

RUSH

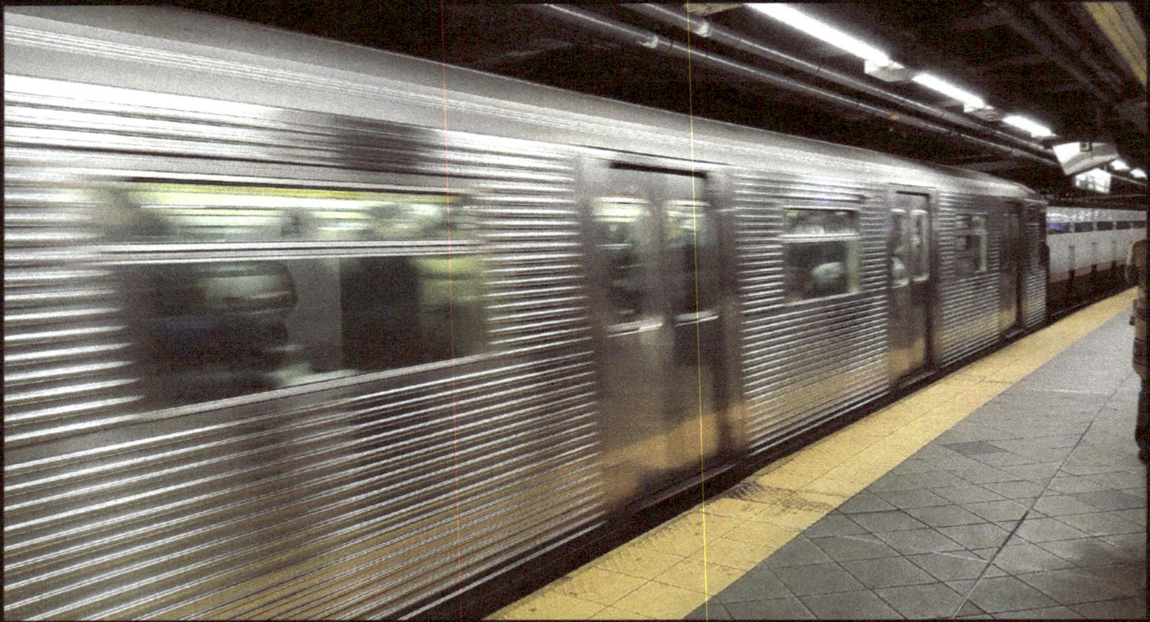

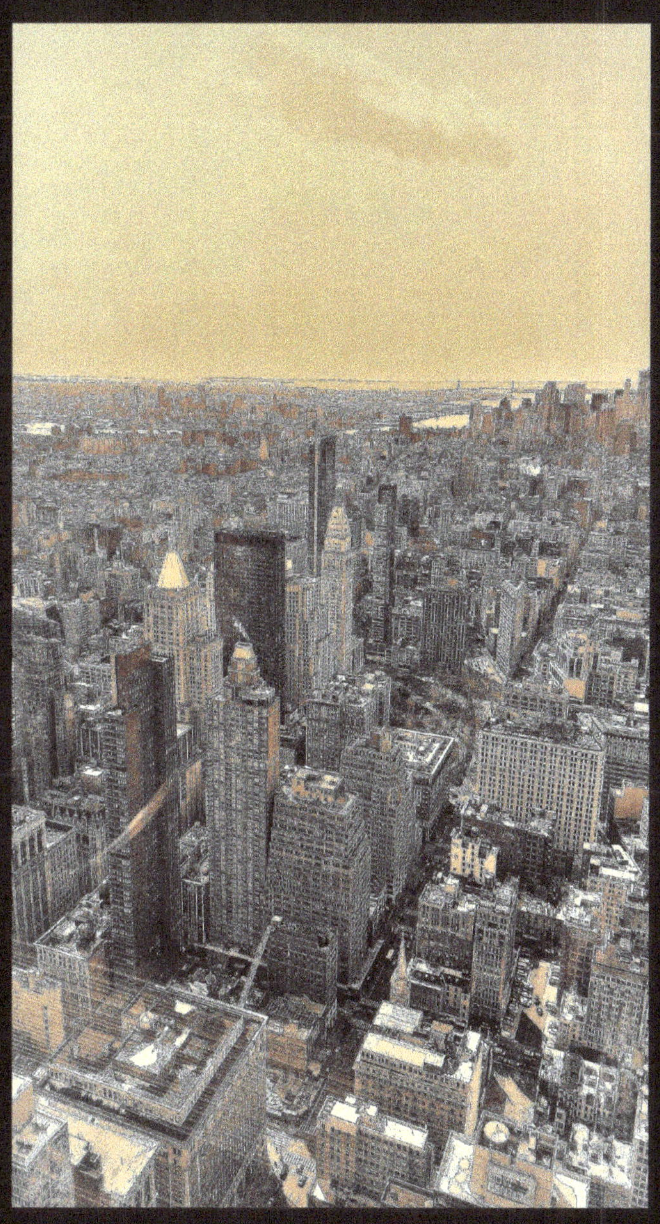

CITRUS TWIST

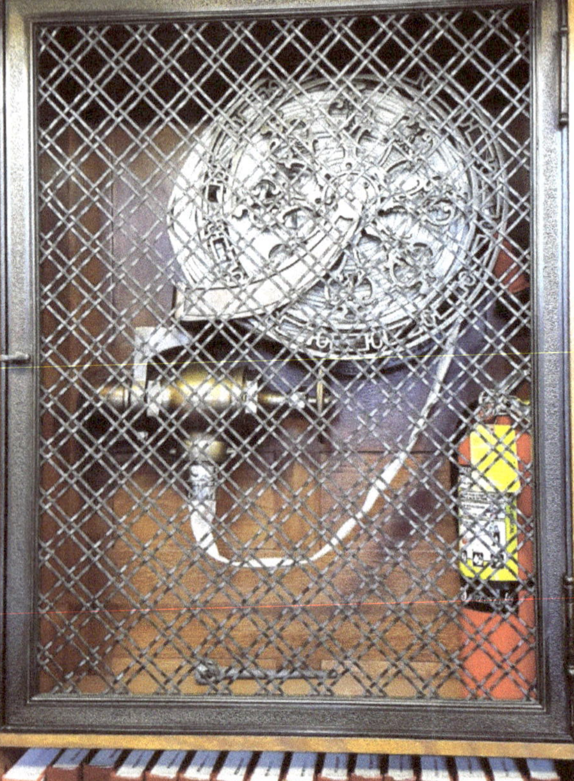

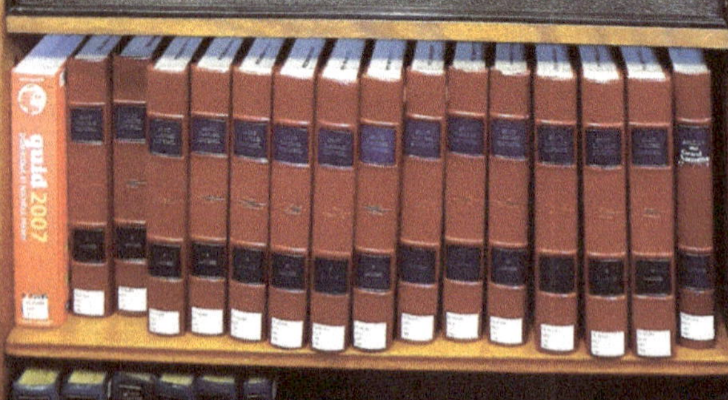

SMOLDER

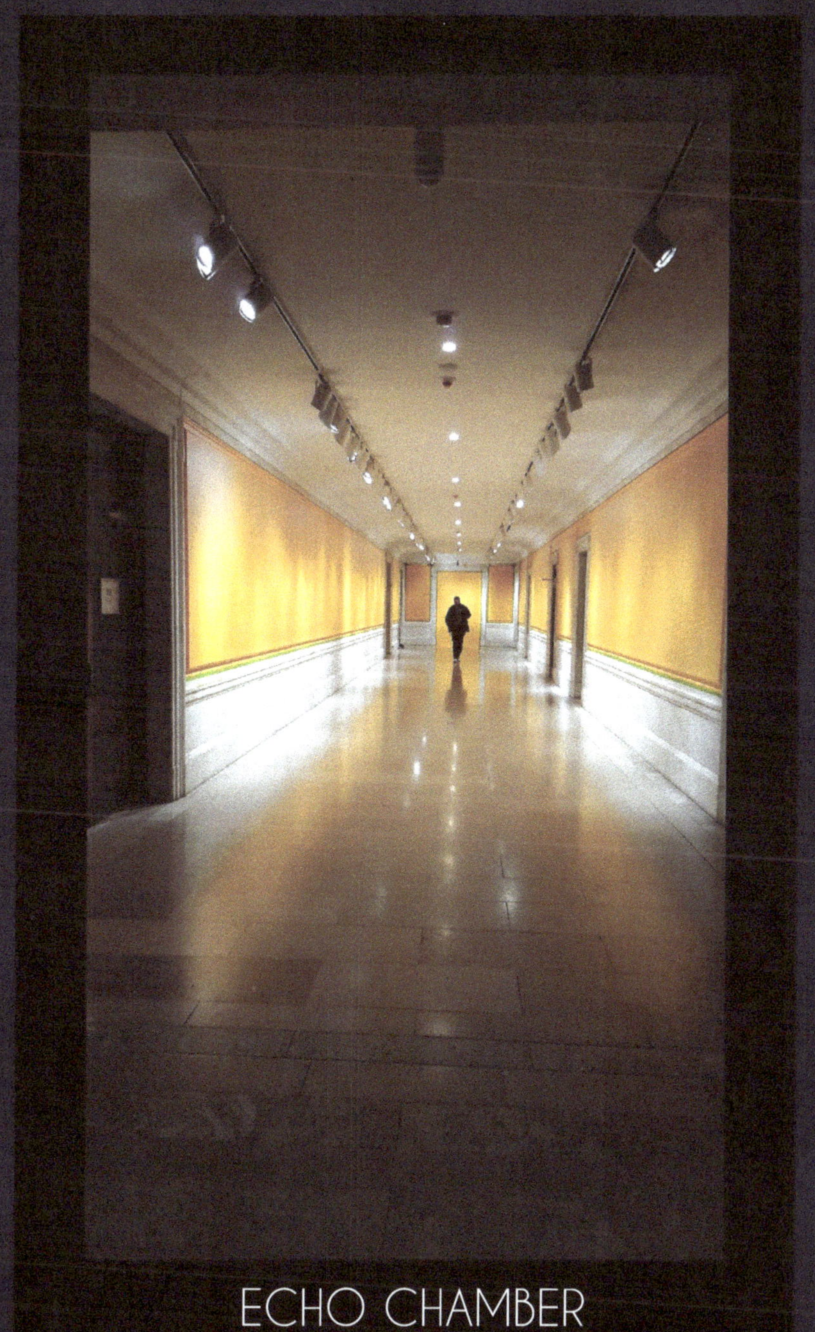

ECHO CHAMBER

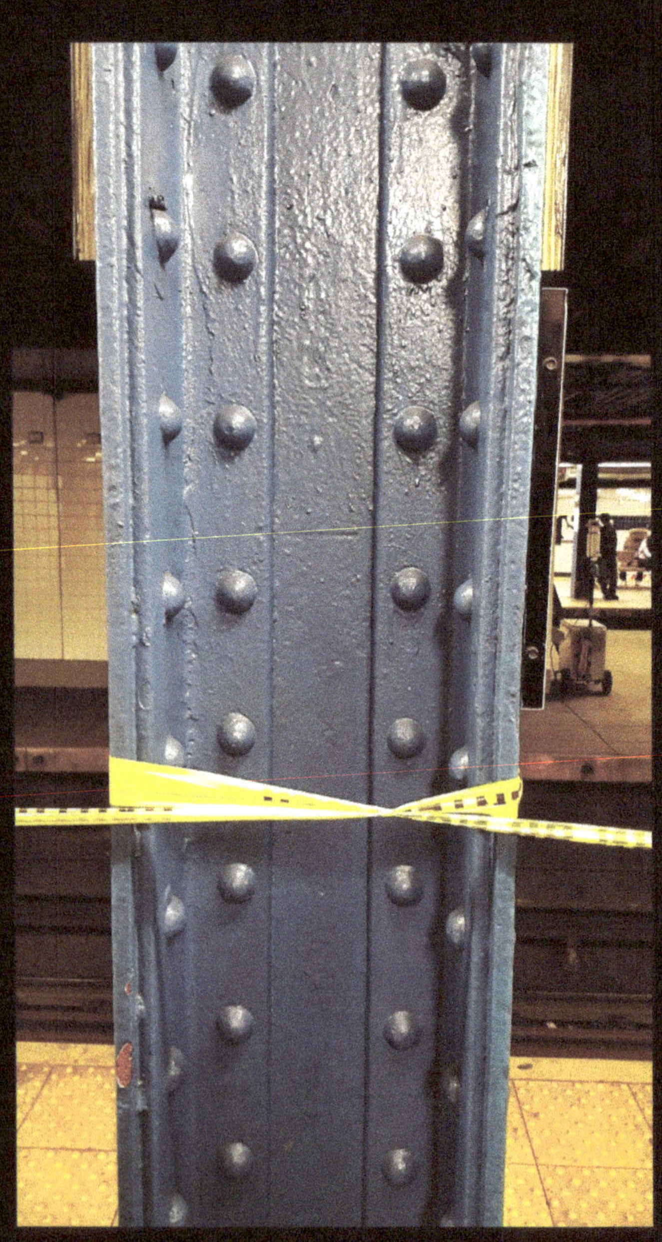

GIFTWRAPPED

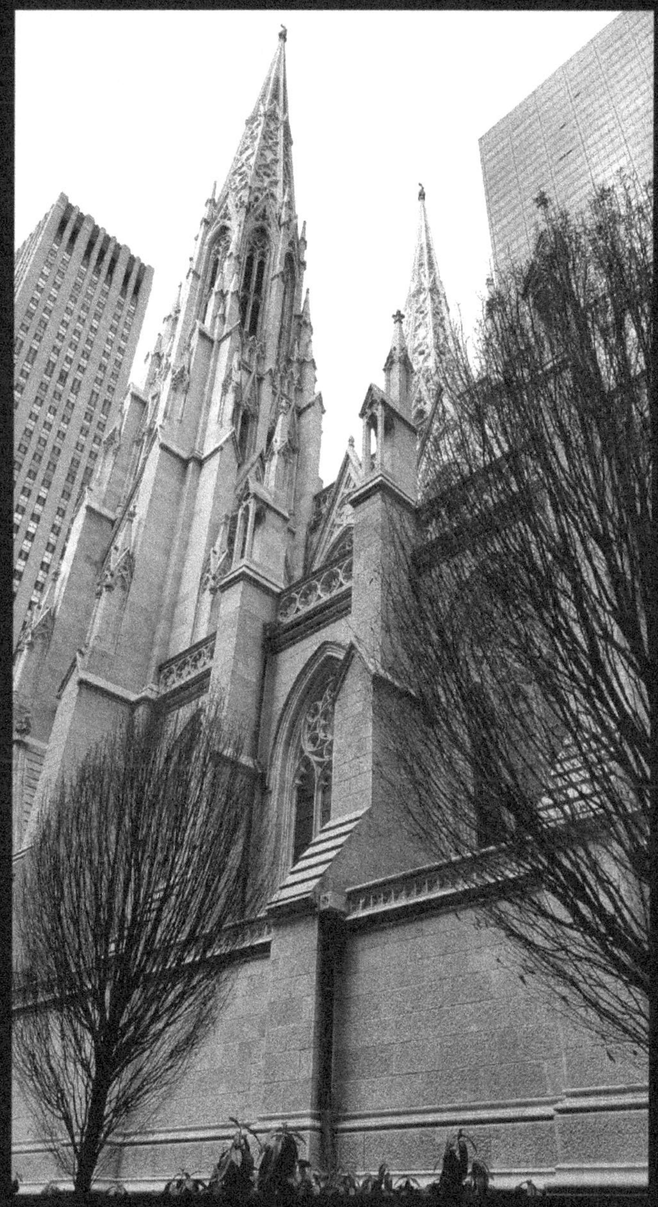

FOREST FOR THE TREES

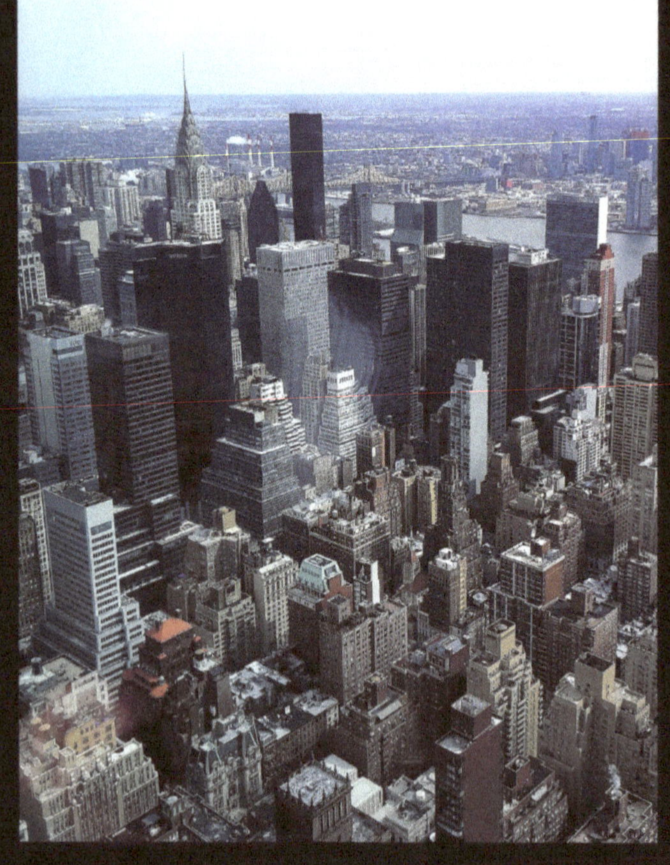

GIZA

Novels

The Family Made of Dust
Winner of Two National Awards
"One of the best novel in ten years."

Beloved
"A deep, dark story with twists and turns."
"Highly recommended."

Reparation
"Beautifully written. The work of a master craftsman."
"Endlessly compelling. A fascinating fusion of forms."

The Travel Photo Art Series

Bikes of Berlin

Necropolises of New Orleans I & II

Ruins of Rome I & II

Ancients of Assisi I & II

Panoramas of Portugal

Nuances of New York

Utopia of the Unicorn

The Zen for Life Series

The Zen of Dogs
Wisdom That Wags the Tail

Zen in the Stable
Wisdom from the Equestrian Life

The Zen of Gardening
Wisdom Rooted in the Earth

The Zen of Chocolate
Wisdom by the Bar

The Zen of Travel
Wisdom from the Journey

The Wisdom for Life Series

The Wisdom of Babies
Life Lessons from the Diaper Set

The Wisdom of Puppies
Puppyhood as a Life Path

The Wisdom of Weddings
Life Lessons from That Special Day

The Beautiful Book Series

The Beautiful Book of Questions

The Beautiful Book for Women

The Beautiful Book for Dream Seekers

The Beautiful Book for Rebels

The Beautiful Book for Lovers

Other Nonfiction by
Laine Cunningham

Woman Alone
A Six-Month Journey Through the Australian Outback

On the Wallaby Track
Essential Australian Words and Phrases

Seven Sisters
Spiritual Messages from Aboriginal Australia

Writing While Female or Black or Gay
Diverse Voices in Publishing

Journals

A selection of blank and lined journals is available in paperback and hardbound versions. The generously sized interior pages are decorated with vintage drawings that alternate in the upper and lower corners. Each two-page spread offers a beautiful place to record your thoughts and wisdom, or capture your world in sketches. They also make great gifts.

Ruins of Rome Journal

Necropolises of New Orleans Journal

Bikes of Berlin Journal

The Zen of Travel Journal

The Zen of Chocolate Journal

The Zen of Gardening Journal

Zen in the Stable Journal

The Zen of Dogs Journal

The Wisdom of Babies Journal

The Wisdom of Weddings Journal

The Wisdom of Puppies Journal

Writing While Female or Black or Gay Journal

Woman Alone Journal

Seven Sisters Journal